Best Approach to: Thesis and Scientific Writing; Methodology and Results

DEDICATION

This work is dedicated to my wife Tanyi Jenet Ama and my son Philip Walters B. A. Tanyi.

Introduction

Writing a thesis is a daunting task that needs a great deal of preparation and research needs to be carried out, be it from grey literature and from qualitative and quantitative sources. During the thesis writing process, a good and effective methodology is needed to help elucidate the finding, which can be shared in the form of a presentation, during the defence of the results of the work done. This book is a practical approach towards thesis writing, and it will walk you through the entire steps in writing an excellent long essay, dissertation or thesis, be it at the degree level, graduate and or post graduate levels.

Chapter 1: How to Write a Thesis

According to University standards, the thesis length is 100 pages and even more (introduction through reference list or bibliography)

Evaluation of thesis will include:

- Length
- Structure
- Presentation
- Content
- Referencing
- In test citation
- Quotations
- Reference list (bibliography)

1.1. Thesis Structure

- Preliminaries
- Chapters
- Conclusion
- References
- Annex(es)

1.2   Content

a. Preliminaries

- Title and cover page
- Second cover page where supervisor signs
- A declaration by the student
- A certification page where the members of the defence jury sign
- Blank page or copyright page (in case of publication)
- Dedication   (NB: no reference to a supreme being)
- Acknowledgements (NB: no reference to a supreme being)
- **Table of Content**
- List of statistical tables

- List of figures (including graphs)
- List of photographic illustrations
- List of abbreviations
- Glossary (brief definition of terms used)
- Abstract (in English and French less than 01 page each, one paragraph)

Exercise (15 minutes):

You have been given some students' theses, evaluate the preliminary section in terms of its

- content
- structure

b. Abstract

It is a brief summary of the work (research) that has been done.

It should include:

- ✓ The key points what, why, how and where of the research;

- ✓ The main research objective, question, hypothesis

- ✓ The background and implication of the study;

- ✓ The research site and population studied;

- ✓ The research methodology (design, variables, sample population & size, data collection and analysis methods and instruments),

- ✓ The main findings and recommendations ;

- ✓ The total time necessary to carry out the research (if necessary);

- ✓ It should have no abbreviations;

- ✓ It should be written in one paragraph only

- ✓ It should be written both in English and French

- ✓ Key words (not more than 05 or 07) at the end

- ✓ It should not be longer than 200 to 300 words

NB: It is the last thing to be written even though it is part of the preliminaries!!!

c. Chapters

Chapter 1

General Introduction

A short introduction (what is the content of the chapter) to the chapter

1.1   Background, Justification and Objectives

1.1.1 Background of the study (context)

> Presentation of the context in which the study is being carried out
>
> Presentation of the historical or geographical frame or context (if necessary)
>
> Highlight the sociological context (different categories of persons or affinities concerned with the problem)

This constitutes what was written in the research proposal (with some modifications if necessary)

NB: If the background is not too long, it should be included in the introduction; if too long it should be put as a separate chapter (chapter 2)

In this case, the research justification becomes the 1ˢᵗ issue in this chapter.

1.1.2   Justification for the research (academic, sociological, moral, spiritual).

This is the introductory part of the research proposal

Conclusions should announce the objectives

1.1.3   Research Objectives

> A short introductory sentence

1.1.3.1 Global Objective

It should be one sentence only

1.1.3.2 Specific Objectives

02 or 03 maximum

These are presented in action verbs

1.2   Implications of the research

NB: This is what was written in the research proposal

1.3   The Research Problem

This is a combination of the topic and problem statement

The main problem, causes, changes observed & the consequences, and the desired situation (vision)

NB: Conclusion should lead to the research questions

1.4   Research Questions

1.4.1   Main research question

1.4.2   Sub Research questions

1.5   Research Hypotheses

         Main Hypothesis (one phrase)

         Sub hypotheses (02 or 03).

1.6   Presentation of the thesis chapters

         Briefly talk about the content of the different chapters by précising the main sub headings of each

         chapter.

Exercise (20 minutes):

In groups read through the students' theses that have been given to you evaluate the

introductory chapter in terms of its:

- **Structure (verify whether all the elements discussed above are included)**
- **Abstract (is it well written?)**
- **Content (is it clear and understandable?)**
- **Presentation (is it catchy, attractive, good etc.)**

NB: If the background to the study is a separate chapter, then it is chapter 2 and literature

review chapter 3.

Chapter 2 Literature Review and Theoretical or Conceptual Framework

- Definition of terms (if not included in the glossary) and concepts
- Specification of what other scholars have written concerning the concept
- Highlight the link between the scholars' work and the research topic so as to establish
  the pertinence and reasons for the study.

NB: the literature review should be presented as follows:

- Author
- Title of the literature read and year of publication
- Summary of what it says in relation to the research in question
- Make reference to what one or two scholars have said

Not necessary to be included in the thesis — It makes the work repetitive

- 30 literature summaries are needed at the list for an MSc.

Chapter 3 (or 4): Methodology

This section concerns presentation and justifications (procedure, reasons etc.) for the methodological approach used in the research. It includes:

3.1 Research design

3.2 Variables and indicators

3.3 Choice of research site & selection criteria

3.4 Sampling design

3.5 Data collection methods & their measurements, instruments and method of administration

3.6 Data analysis methods

3.7 An idea about the presentation of your results

3.8 the difficulties encountered and limitations of the research

- Difficulties in application of the methods and how you went about them
- General difficulties (logistics, accommodation, study site, instruments, health etc.) that influenced the research work and the results

3.9 The scope of the research and the areas/issues not included in the research

Exercise (30 minutes):

Read through the literature review and methodology chapters and discuss:

  i.   **the pertinence of the literature cited in the literature review chapter**

  ii.   **the manner of in-text citation in the literature review chapter**

  iii.   **the coherence of the ideas discussed in the literature review chapter**

  iv.   **the structure of the methodology chapter**

  v.   **the content of each aspect of the methodology chapter (clarity, easily understood)**

  vi.   **are there variables and indicators for each variable**

  vii.   **the methods of data collection and analysis:**

      a. **are they useful for the research in question**

      b. **can they be replicated**

  viii.   **Is there a scope and limitation of each research, as well as difficulties encountered?**

Chapter 4 (5): Critical Analysis of the Research Data (Results and Discussions)

A short introduction to the chapter

4.1 Presentation and interpretation of the Results

NB: Do not present any results (tables, graphs, pictures etc.) without précising what they are and do not repeat the information contained in them, but say what they mean.

4.2 Discussions

In reference to each main result:

Make reference to the literature cited in the literature review and introductory chapters to either confirm an idea being discussed or giving a contrary view.

Say what is it that you are contributing as a new idea to the existing body of knowledge

NB: In this chapter, the results and discussions could either be presented separately or together.

Chapter 5 (6): Evaluation of the Research Question and Hypotheses and Recommendations (include areas for further research)

a) Evaluation (examination) of the research problem and hypotheses
- Restate the research objectives (main and specific)
- For each specific objective, restate the corresponding research question and hypothesis (es)
- Cross examine the research hypotheses and either reject of accept it, and answer the research question
- Draw conclusions

b) Recommendations

These are made from the conclusions drawn through the cross examinations of the research hypothesis and answers to the research question(s)

6 (7). Conclusions

What are the learning points or what is the take home message. It should contain the following elements (all written in paragraph form):
- A brief summary of the justification for the research (one paragraph, 03 to 04 lines)
- A recall of the research objectives
- A recall of the research problem (03 to 04 lines)
- A recall of the research questions and or hypotheses
- A brief summary of the main research findings
- **Validation or not of the research hypotheses**
- **Answers to the research questions (main, sub)**
- A brief summary of the main recommendations
- A small general conclusion

Include areas for further research

Exercise:

Read through the thesis conclusion and evaluate it in terms of its content and structure

5. References (Bibliography) **using the Harvard referencing Style**

Exercise:

Read through the chapters on presentations of results and discussion, evaluation of research questions and hypotheses, and conclusions and evaluate in terms of their:

     i.   structure

     ii.   content

     iii.   the clarity of the information or message in the content (context).

     iv.   the referencing style

6. Annexes

- Sample research instrument(s) used
- Maps and graphs that are too cumbersome
- Other pictures
- Other important items (research budget, etc.) that can permit future researchers to emulate.

5. Tips for writing a thesis, term paper or paper for publication

Formats and Layouts

  A. Margins

     i.   3cm from the left   } to permit binding

     ii.   2 to 2.5 cm on the right

     iii.   Justify all right margins, check and adjust hyphenations

     iv.   Top and bottom margins: 2 cm to 2.5cm each

  B. Line Spacing

     i.   Interline : 1½ spacing or 1.5 cm

     ii.   Indented block quotations, footnotes, itemised lists, reference lists, table of content, lists of tables & illustrations, subheadings etc. are in single spacing or 01cm.

  C. Indention

     i.   Be consistent in paragraph or block quotations indenting

     ii.   Block quotations should leave larger spaces on the left and right as compared to paragraph indents

  D. Thesis parts

     i.   Preliminaries (front matter)

ii.   Text (introduction, chapters, conclusion)

iii.   Back matter (references & annexes)

Each part has various sections. Begin each section on a new page.

E. Pagination

i.   Preliminaries: lowercase roman numerals e.g. i, ii, iv, ix, xi

ii.   Text and Back matter: Arabic numerals e.g. 1, 2, 3, 4

iii.   All preliminaries page numbers are centred and placed at the bottom of the page

iv.   All Arabic numerals page numbers are either:

- centred and placed at the bottom of the page or

- centred and placed at the bottom of pages that bear titles and centred at the top or at the right hand corner of all the other pages.

v.   Preliminaries such as title page, blank or copyright page, dedication page, epigraph (quotation placed at the beginning of a thesis) page and table of content pages, even though counted, may or may not necessarily have page numbers written on them.

F. Capitalisation

i.   Only major headings should be put in Uppercase characters

ii.   Sub headings should have sentence case characters (Upper and Lowercase).

The American style specifies that all first letters of words be put in Upper case

G. Character or Font Size

12 Times New Romans, etc.

For major headings, font size 14 and most often put in bold or highlighted.

H. Chapter heads and other major headings

i.   Put chapter heads in Capital letters and the 1st letters of each word in major sub headings

I. In-text citation and reference list (bibliography) should follow the Harvard Referencing style that has been discussed lengthily in the section on research proposal writing.

Chapter 2: How to Prepare an Oral Presentation

An oral presentation refers to communicating your research results to an audience either at international or national meetings and conferences.

a) Importance of making a presentation:

- An opportunity to communicate your research findings;
- An opportunity to make valuable contacts;
- An opportunity to enhance your reputation.

b) **Your presentation depends on**:

- What your message is;
- Who your audience is.
- Background, interest

c) **You have something to say**

- say it with authority;
- be enthusiastic about your topic.

1) Types of oral presentations

- seminar presentations;
- workshop presentations;
- Thesis defense presentations;
- scientific meeting presentations.
- National conferences
- International conferences

2) Features of a scientific meeting and thesis defense

- Varied audience and therefore mixed interest;
- Audience speaks and listens in a foreign language;

- Abstract not always read in advance;
- Strict time schedule
- 10 to 12 minutes presentation
- 3 to 5 minutes discussion

3) Features of an oral presentation

- Attractive;
- Interesting;
- Well structured;
- Easy to understand;
- Have a clear message;
- Focus on the main message

4) Features of a good presentation

- Audience adapted;
- Brief;
- Clear;
- Devoted;
- Enthusiastic;
- Flexible (adapt to failures etc.)

5) Preparing the Oral Presentation

- Audience has different perspectives;
- How best to raise and maintain audience's attention and interest;
- How best to structure the topic to facilitate audience understanding and remember your take-home message?

5) Audience attention

- Beginning
  - Audience attention is high, people are curious about what you will say;
- Middle
  - Audience attention is low, people have their own thoughts. Introduce interesting things to maintain their attention

- End
    - o Audience attention is high, people are curious about the conclusions

6) What to do in the beginning

- Inviting and informative title
    - o State a problem, pose a question, make a conclusion
    - o Make the title provocative
- Announce the objective before you start
    - o The objective of this talk (or presentation) is to…

- Acknowledge colleagues, funding, institutions etc.
- Give a general structure for your talk using IMRAD – C format
    - o Introduction
    - o Materials and methods
    - o Results and discussions
    - o Conclusions
- Know your audience
    - o Know their background or level
    - o Bring them up to a level
    - o Aim your talk at that level

7) What to do in the Middle of your presentation

- Vary the tone of your voice
- Loud/soft, fast/slow
- Vary the style of your talk
- Read, quote, be spontaneous, have dialogue, ask for questions, move around
- Vary the visuals of your talk
- Text, tables, equations, charts, clip art animation
- Anticipate audience questions
- Include questions/answers in your talk
- How did we do it? We simply…
- Bring the audience along with you
- "Now think with me about this" etc.
- Use examples to explain difficult concepts

- Interpret results
- Ask audience for questions

8) What to do at the end of a presentation

- Summarise your main findings;
- Explain practical significance;
- Give recommendations;
- Provide some points for discussion;
- Last slide should contain your take-home message;
- Do not forget the take-home message;
- Do not run out of time.

9) Coping with questions

- Questions show interest, leave enough time for questions when presenting;
- Take down questions;
- Listen carefully to the question and make positive comments;
- "Thank you for that question"
- In the case of thesis presentation: "Thank you honourable member of the jury"
- Answer the question
- Repeat, rephrase, clarify the question for those who didn't hear it;
- Address short answers to the entire audience;
- Avoid a dialogue or discussion with any member of the audience except in the case of thesis defence;
- "let us talk about this at coffee break"
- Avoid jargon or giving technical answers
- Don't be afraid to say,
- I don't know but I can find out and e-mail you (not in the case of course seminars and thesis or long essay defence!!!)

10) Visuals Support for your Presentation

- Where you can, use a figure, table, chart etc. instead of words
- People retain information more when it is communicated to them in words and figures (pictures, charts, graphs etc.) than with either words or figures alone.

11) Which Visuals to Use

- Know what equipment is available;
- Computer, projector, pointer, remote control, microphone
- Learn how to use available equipment before making a presentation;
- Check the compatibility of the equipment;
- Know the illumination of the room;
- Darken room light for slides
- With illuminated room the audience can:
    - See you better and you can see them better
    - See to make notes
    - Not get tired so easily
- If you have to turn the lights off, be sure to turn them back on as soon as possible

12) Electronic Presentation

- Professional presentation
    - Use bullets, animation, hyperlinks

        ..\Harvard Referencing style.doc

        ..\Harvard Referencing style.doc
    - Animation can be distracting, so do not vary so much of it
- Make last minute changes easily;
- Hide slides until needed;
- Room can be illuminated;
- Be sure the equipment is compatible;
- Prepare back-ups: CD, USB, hard copy, etc. in case of failure.

13) Creating Visuals

- Choose colours that emphasize message;
- Use harmonising and contrasting colours;
    - Avoid red – green comparisons
- Use colours that allow room lights;
- Use dark text on light background;

    I am going to school

    I am going to school
- Use clip art for attractive visuals, but don't let it be a distraction

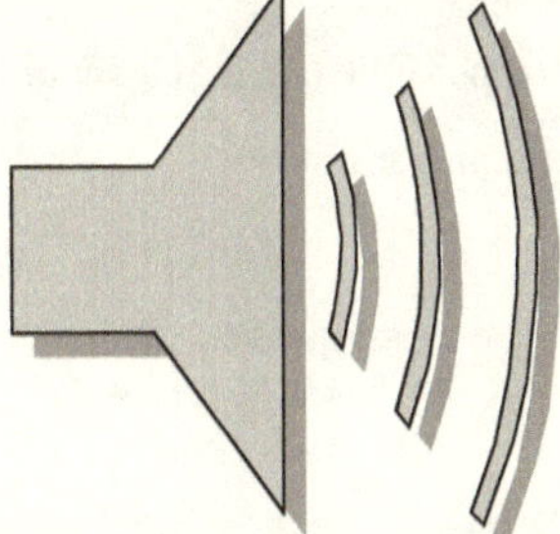

17

- Keep it (the display) simple;
- Use large text font;
- Don't overload;
- Face the audience.

14) Writing text

- Simple and easy to understand;
- Use bullets to accentuate text (but do not vary the type of bullets so much)
  - Man
  - Woman
  - Children
  - Animal
  - cat etc.
- Use large font
  - Text minimum font is 24 points for a power point presentation but can reduce it to 20
  - Heading font is 40 points (but you can reduce it to 32 depending on the size of the room)
- Use italics, bold or both for emphasis

15) Spacing

- Apply Rule of 5s
  - Maximum 5 lines per slide
  - Maximum 5 words per line
  - Split up slides if they get too busy and words become smaller
  - Animate slide if it contains supporting information and therefore becomes too busy.

16) Making Tables and Charts

- Keep tables and charts simple
  - Round off numbers if possible e.g. 2.567 should be 2.6
- Use only 02 or 03 rows, columns or lines
- Use large font size
- Give a summary that sends the message to the audience

For example

Table 1: Crop Yield by Variety and Year

Variety	Crop Yield (5kg)			
	Year			
	1980	1990	2000	2010
A	75	275	250	375
B	50	150	140	175
C	20	50	30	60
- 5% to 10% decrease in 2000. Variety C yields lowest .				

Types of Charts

- Scatter chart to show dispersal

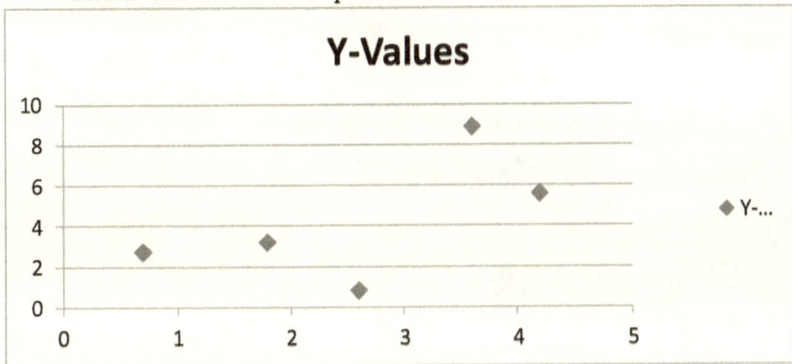

- Line chart to show continuous trendline

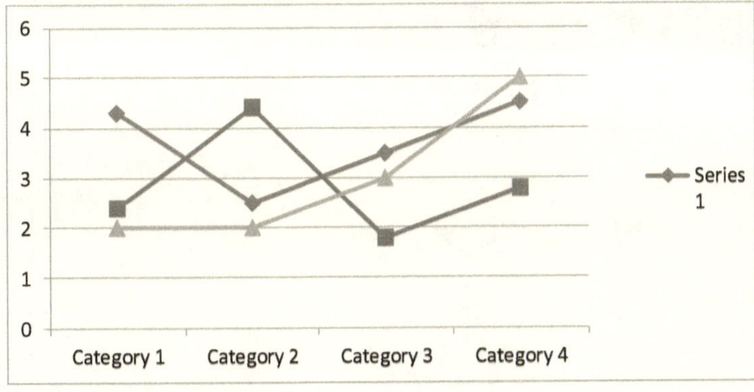

Bar Chart or histogram to show discrete comparisons

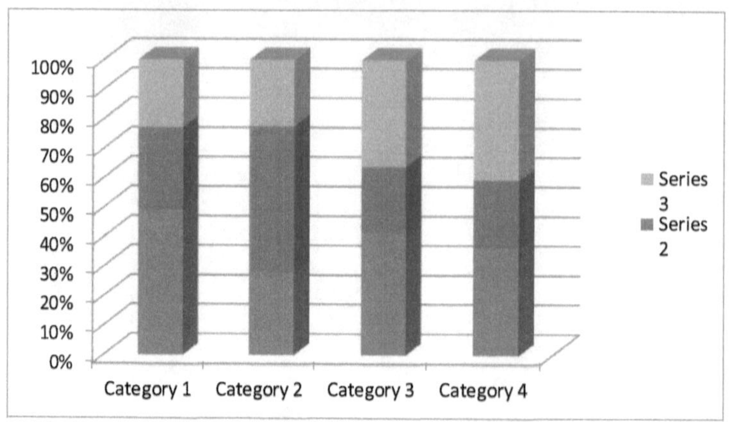

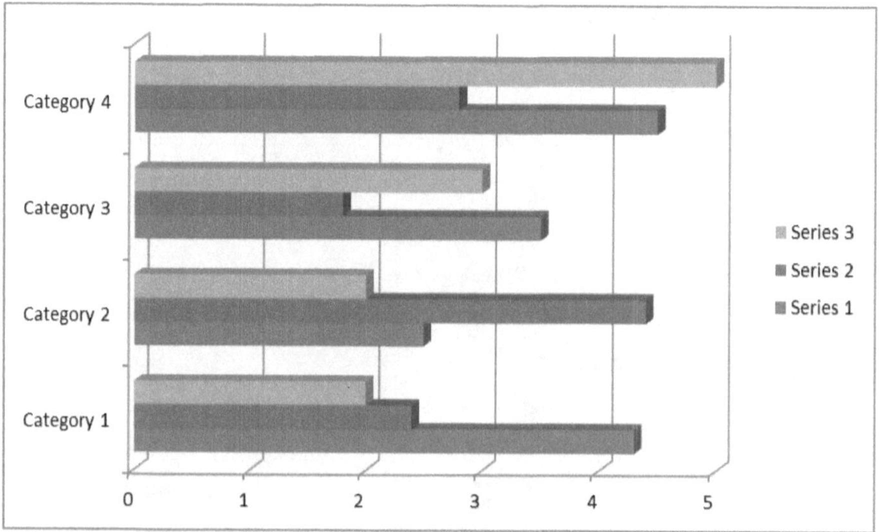

Pie chart to show proportions

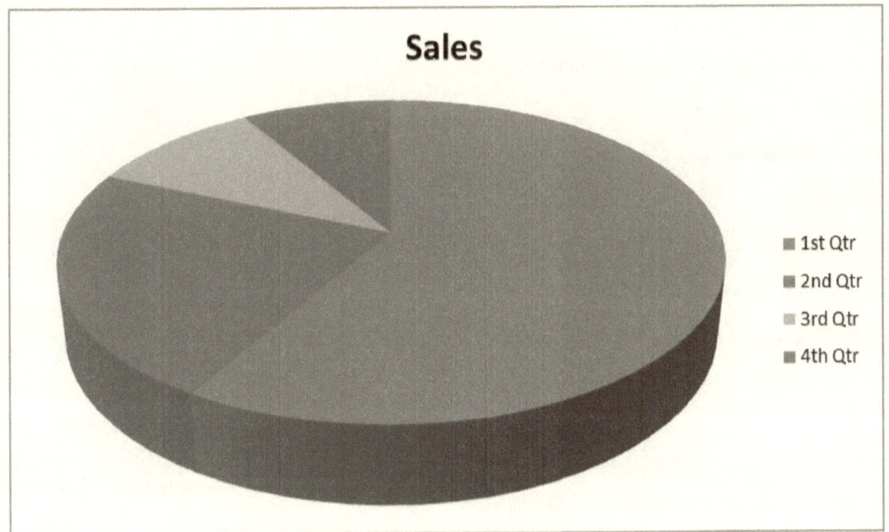

Mixed chart to show data with trend line (mostly used in regression analysis)

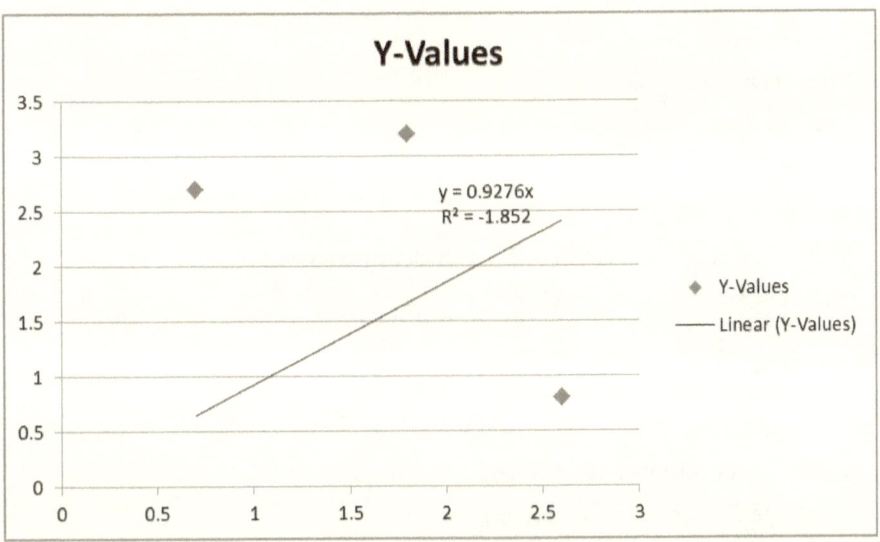

I) How to perform during a presentation

- Control nervousness;
    - Know your subject
    - Be well prepared
    - Take in a deep breath before starting
    - Control your hands if nervous
    - Don't jingle money or keys in your pockets etc.
- Be confident, not arrogant;

- Be enthusiastic;
- Thank your chair/host for the introduction;
- Be prepared to introduce yourself;
- Speak slowly and clearly;
- Have good visuals;
- Respect time;
- Questions could be asked during your talk or later;
- Your dressing should not distract the audience;
- Be careful when using a laser pointer;
- Don't read your talk from your computer
    - Ties you to the lectern
    - Makes you lose eye contact with audience
    - Visuals may help you out
- Use notes
    - Print out slides
    - Make comments on slides
    - Use large font
    - Use keywords
- If using microphone, make sure:
    - of the direction of the sound to enable enough transmission
    - You know how to turn it on and off

II) Have an exit strategy

- How to end your talk
    - Thank you for your attention. I will be happy to answer any questions.
    - Thank you for listening. Are there any questions?
    - Questions? Thank you for listening
    - Thank you for listening. Questions?
    - Respectable honourable members of the jury, this is the end of my presentation. I am ready for questioning (in the case of thesis or long essay defence).

NB: Address the thesis defence jury as "Respectable Honourable members of Jury"

Chapter 3: How to Write a Scientific Paper

It refers to communicating science to others.

The discussions in this section focus on important techniques for effective writing.

The issues to be discussed include:

- ❖ A scientific article (paper);
- ❖ Coherence;
- ❖ Choice of words;
- ❖ Active, Tight writing;
- ❖ Parallel structure;
- ❖ Transitions to link ideas;
- ❖ Correct grammar;
- ❖ Punctuation;
- ❖ Preparation of tables and figures;
- ❖ Writing statistics.

3.1.   Structure of a scientific paper

- Title
- Abstract
- Introduction
- Materials and methods
- Results & Discussion
- Discussion
- Conclusions or Implications
- Acknowledgements
- References
- Appendix

3.1.1   Title

- Descriptive or declarative

  - Descriptive: tells the objective of the research to the reader

  - Declarative: tells the results or conclusion of the research to the reader

- A good title tells what the paper is about

  - Informative: describes the subject and gives what is (object) studied e.g. Mating behaviour in pigs

Not informative: Mating behaviour

- Specific: Differentiates the research from other research on the subject

  e.g. Dominance behaviour of large white pig race

  Not specific: Dominance behaviour of pigs

- Concise: says only what is necessary (7 to 10 words)

  e.g. Sperm transport, storage and capacity in beef cattle.

  Wrong: Studies on the reproductive biology in bulls including sperm transport, sperm storage and sperm capacity

  e.g. Effects of feeding on milk production of Mediterranean buffaloes

- Use a title that suggests the structure of the paper

  Example: A Mathematical Model for the Lactation Curve in Dairy Cows

- Can use two-part or "hanging" titles

  - Two-part title:

  Example: Persistence of lactation yield: A novel approach

  - Hanging title (mostly used in review articles)

  Example: Lactation curves in Dairy Goats.

- Suggestions for title beginnings

Effect(s) of ....   Estimation of........   Comparison of........   Measurement of.....

Influence of ....   Prediction of........   Use of...............   Modelling the ....

Evaluation of ......   Control of...........   Evidence of........

Efficacy of........   Application of........   Impact of...........

- Avoid using waste words

Observation(s) of....   Investigation(s) of.......Research on.......   Preliminary study of....

Studies of.......   Examination of........   Note about

- Avoid titles with a series e.g. I, II, III, or 1, 2, 3 unless papers are submitted as a set

  - Looks like showing up

- Inability to push subsequent papers

3.1.2   Abstract

- ❖ Start with motivation or justification (only if there is enough room for word limitation, if not, leave out)

- ❖ State the objective, aim or purpose of the research;

- ❖ Summarise important materials and methods;

- ❖ Summarise important (main) results;

- ❖ End with important conclusions and impact;

- ❖ The abstract should stand alone: no references, no abbreviations;

- ❖ Should either be indicative or informative

  - o Indicative:

    - Indicates the objectives of the research and suggests results in general terms

    - Makes the reader want to read the paper because it might be interesting

  - o Informative:

    - States objectives and supports conclusions with data

    - Makes the reader want to read the paper because it is interesting.

- ❖ End abstract with key words (03 to 07 words).

3.1.3.   Introduction

The introduction should be short, concise, clear and coherent.

What to include:

- Motivate and justify the research

  - o include preview of study site and subjects if applicable (a short paragraph: 04 to 05 lines);

  - o The scientific orientation which includes the main problem or issue at stake, its consequences and desired situation

NB: In the case of a thesis, it is a brief summary of the research justification and the problem statement.

- State what has been done (summarise the relevant literature)

- State what has **Not** been done (specify the knowledge gap)

- State main objective, question and hypothesis (specifies what is the point of the research)

- Give a preview of the materials and methods

- Give a preview of the results

3.1.4.   Materials and Methods

It refers to a description of the methodology (materials and methods) used for the research.

This section should:

- Include enough information but not more than necessary so that the research can be repeated
- Give a clear and complete description for the materials and analytical and statistical procedures
    - Organise methods logically
    - Use specific and informative language

3.1.5. Results

It refers to presenting the research findings.

- Summarise and illustrate the findings logically
- use tables and figures if necessary
- If tables and figures are used, refer to these in the text
- Do not repeat numbers in the text that are in the tables, rather give an explanation of the tables.
- If tables and figures are used, describe findings with support from them

    Ex: body weights of individuals averaged 3 kg (Table 1).

NB: It is easier to read articles that interweave results and discussions in one section. However, separating results from discussions or not depends on the Journal where the research is to be published.

3.1.7. Discussion

It involves:

- Interpretation of the results
- It supports one's conclusions with comparisons and contrasts from the literature
- Recognises negative results
- Describes limitations of the research

3.1.8. Conclusions

- Explain the main results of the research in terms of the objectives
- Describe what the results mean for the society
- Give implications in non-jargon language
    - Specify the research impact.

3.1.9. Acknowledgements

Start with:

- General acknowledgement
    - Institution(s) or laboratory
    - Research project
    - Source of funds
- Specific acknowledgement
    - Supervisor, colleagues and technicians (field assistance etc.)
    - The interviewees (respondents)
    - Reviewer
- Dedication (if possible, but not very necessary).

3.1.10. References

- Follow the instructions of the Journal

  Ex: (Name, Year) or Name (Year)

  (Name, Number) or Name (Number)

- Be certain:
    - All references cited in text are listed
    - All references listed are cited in text

3.1.11. Appendix

Provides supplemental material

- Numerical examples
- Details of analytical procedures
- Novel computer programmes
- Mathematical proofs
- Etc.

3.2.   Conditions for Effective Writing (This is also applicable to a research proposal and a thesis)

- ❖ Clear: reader gets the message
- ❖ Complete: answers reader's questions

❖ Correct: the message is accurate

❖ Efficient: saves reader's time

Avoid reader spending time to understand the sense of the research;

A clue should be arrived at when reading the work.

3.3 Coherence

It refers to the logical sequence of sentences within a paragraph or between paragraphs.

It is the link or thread that takes the reader from one idea to the next.

It constitutes a major problem in scientific writing and must be avoided.

To improve on coherence:

- ✓ Put similar topics together to avoid jumbling up and repetition of ideas; and

- ✓ Discuss one idea per paragraph

    - State the main idea in a "topic sentence" : tell the reader what the paragraph is about

    - Put topic sentence first in a paragraph

    - Develop the idea of the topic sentence

    - Keep your paragraphs short

- ✓ End a sentence with a "new" idea that is to be discussed in the next sentence;

- ✓ Start a sentence with an "old" idea that was announced at the end of the previous sentence

    Example: After **insemination**, spermatozoa are stored in the hen and slowly released. After release, spermatozoa are captured so that fertilisation of an oocyte can occur up to four weeks after insemination.

- ✓ The writing style should be consistent

    - o Use the same word for the same idea

        - experiment
        - Trial
        - study

        do not use these interchangeably in an article, even though they may mean the same thing.

    - o Use the same organisational pattern for successive sentences and paragraphs

- ✓ Use parallel structure

3.4 Parallel Structure

It refers to using the same grammatical form and sentence pattern to express ideas that have the same logical function

Importance:

- Smooth writing

- More forceful writing

- Balances sentences

- Easy understanding

In parallel structure:

- Use *than* or *as* when doing comparison

  Ex: For breed A, weaning weight *was lower for* calves on Diet 1 *than* on Diet 2.

- Use whereas or however when making a contrast between ideas

  Ex: For Breed A, weaning weight *was lower for* calves on Diet 1 *than* on Diet 2, *whereas* the rate of weight gain was faster for calves on Diet 1 than on Diet 2.

  Ex2: For Breed B, *however*, weaning weight *was higher for* calves on Diet 1 *than* on Diet 2, *whereas* the rate of weight gain *was slower for* calves on Diet 1 *than* on Diet 2.

- Balance nouns with nouns; (ad)verbs with (ad)verbs

- Items in a list or series must have the same construction

  - Donor cows were synchronised, inseminated, and sacrificed

  - Donor cows were synchronised by…., were inseminated by…., and were sacrificed by…

3.5.   Verb Tenses

The verb tense used depends on the type of ideas discussed:

- For ideas related to motivation and justification, use present tense

  Ex: Feed is the largest expense in the production of pigs

- For literature review, use past or present perfect tense

  Ex: Studies showed that pigs *were* or the pig *was*….

- In presenting the research objectives, use past tense

  Ex: The objective was to model the growth of….

- In presenting the materials and methods, use past tense

  Ex: Data *were* collected; Data *were* analysed

- In presenting research results and Discussions, use past and present tenses

  Ex: Growth *was* faster for pigs than for goats, which *means* that pigs respond faster to hormonal changes than goats.

- In making reference to tables and figures, use present tense

- In making conclusions, use present tense

  Ex: results *suggest* that….

3.6   Making one's work easy to read

3.6.1. Choice of words

Choose the right words:

- Use words that are accurate
  - That say what you mean
  - The reader should not guess

- Use appropriate words
  - That fit well with other words
  - Write for the reader and not for the writer

- Use familiar words
  - That are easy to understand
  - The reader should not have to use the dictionary

3.6.2. Avoid Jargon

- Use technical terms only when necessary
- Use plain language
  - Instead of to ascertain the potential application, write to find out the use of…
- Write simply
  - Use shorter and more common words

3.6.3. Passive and Active form of verb

- Passive form: the subject is acted upon

Ex: Cows were bred by technicians using artificial insemination

Use passive form of verb to:

- Provide coherence within a paragraph
  - Transitions between sentences by repeating a word

    Ex: the epidemic ended with the discovery of a vaccine. The vaccine was developed by..

- Omit an unknown or irrelevant agent

  Ex: data were analysed by regression

➢ Active form of verb: The subject does the action

Ex: Technicians bred cows using artificial insemination

- Active form of verb is:

    - Shorter, clearer, more vigorous, more interesting, less boring, more direct, more forceful, easier to understand, more efficient, less pompous and less bureaucratic.

- Use more often active verb than passive verb in situations where:

    - The subject discussed is used in the sentence

        Ex: Miller (1999) has shown that….

        Not: It has been shown by Miller (1999) that….

    - The sentence begins with It

        Ex: These results suggested that…..

        Not: It was inferred from these results that….

3.7   Designing Effective Visuals (Tables and Figures)

Tables and figures are visual presentations of data that:

➢ Help make numbers meaningful and convey information

➢ Show relationships

➢ Emphasise and present material more concisely

3.7.1   Tables

Tables are used to:

➢ Organise and compress data into a standardised form

➢ Focus on specific data or estimates

➢ Emphasize similarities and differences

- Group similar items

- Separate dissimilar items

Tables should:

- Have titles that explain the issues presented in the table.

    Ex: Table1: Mean Body-Weight Gain (g) by Breed and Diet

- Be Accurate and easy to read

- Have enough spacing, ruling, arrangement of headings and placement with respect to the text

- Be legible
    - Sentence case (Upper and Lower case)
    - Use common units
    - Avoid vertical lines between columns in very large tables (Use a vertical line after every five columns)
    - Avoid horizontal lines except when necessary.
    - Space after every 5 items
- Follow a logical format
    - Portrait or landscape orientation
- Use N/D in empty cells to mean "no data", "not detectable", or "not determined"
- Arrange comparisons vertically for ease of comparability
- Have concise content
- Avoid repetitive information
- Avoid redundant information (exclude data that can be computed in the text)
    - For example: mean and coefficient of variation, sometimes STD
- Have footnotes where applicable (source, key to the content)
    - Avoid explanations of results as footnotes.
- Be self-content (stand-alone). Copy definitions into the table to facilitate understanding.
- Not have abbreviations e.g. qty, Amt (amount)
- Avoid presenting data in an array of raw data, but use percentages, proportions
- Be numbered with an Arabic numeral and given a title
- Table numbering should respect the order in which the tables are mentioned in the text
- Number tables in the appendix (annex) separately from the tables in the text. E.g. A1, A2, A3
- Each table should be placed as close as possible after the first reference to it
- In the case of a continued table (occupy more than 01 page), repeat the column headings on each page), indicate the source and footnote at the end of the table.

Statistical tables

These are tables that present information in numerical form:

- Percentages (%)
- Tallies of occurrences (frequencies)
- Amounts of money
- Proportions
- Etc.

NB: For ease of comparison, do not present an array of raw data (figures), but use percentages or proportions.

When percentages or proportions are used,

> - It is always good to indicate the N – from which the percentages and proportions are derived.
> - N- (Sample size) could either be presented as a separate column or as a separate row.

3.7.2   Figures

Figures refer to all illustrations such as drawings, paintings, photographs, charts, graphs and maps.

Figures are used to focus on general relationships among data or estimates.

Figures should:

> - Have a consistent scale, boldness and font lines (min. 1 pt.)
>> - Character size should be large enough to enable readability after reduction (minimum 8 pt. after reduction)
> - Graphs and charts should be placed as close as possible to their first references in the text
> - Should be referred to by numbers so that their exact placement is flexible
>> - Some Journals decide to group all illustrations together (if they are of one type) and placed at the end of the paper or in the annex (appendix) section.
> - Each figure should be numbered using Arabic numerals and have a caption – title and legend, all placed at the bottom. A legend can be placed by the right side of the figure in the case of graphs and charts.
> - Avoid unnecessary background or gridlines
> - Avoid crowded or busy figures and "white space"
> - Understood to stand alone or independently to facilitate understanding.

e.g. Figure 5.7: Malende Farmers' Freelisted Cassava Variety Salience by Number of Varieties Grown

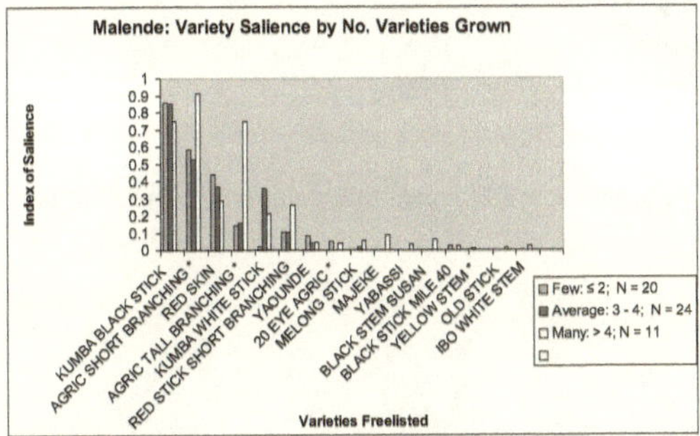

Title placed in the wrong position

Figure 5.8: Koudandeng Farmers' Freelisted Cassava Variety Salience by Number of Varieties Grown in 2007

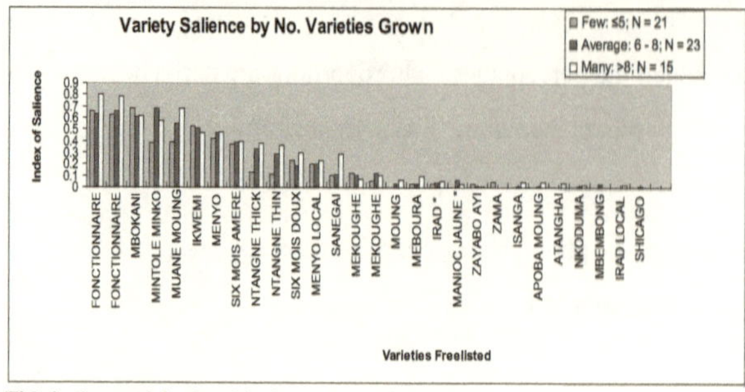

Title in the graph is placed in the wrong position

> If figure has multiple parts, number as follows: figure 1A, 1B, 1c etc.

Pie charts

Used to:

> Compare a segment of data with the whole data

- Limit segments to 5 – 7

- Label segments outside or inside the circle (depends on the software programme)

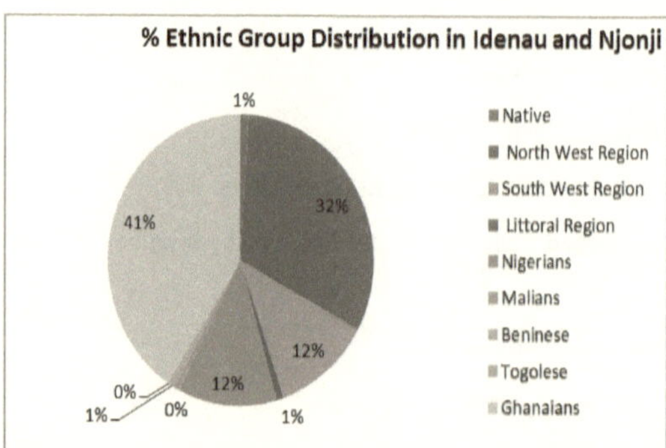

Exploded pie charts are not logical ways of organising and presenting data. It is difficult to tell where the different segments separate.

Bar charts or histograms

Are used to compare one item with the other

> Place bars in logical order

> Place labels inside or outside, not both

> Avoid 3-D bar charts, unless 3-D data is used. These are hard to make sense out of;

> Avoid "stacked" effect (unclear blank spaces) by starting the Y-axis with a number other than zero.

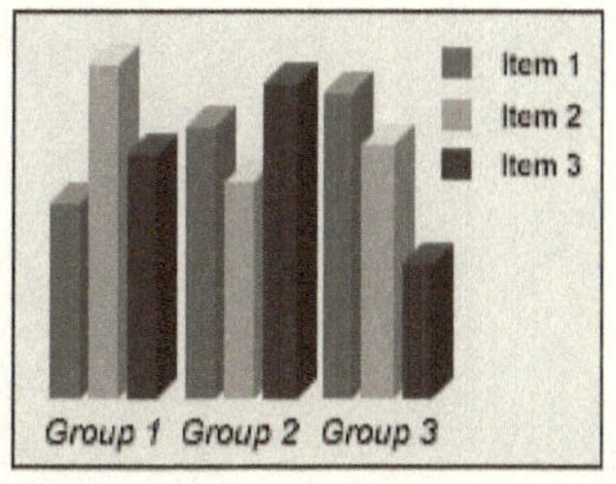

Vertical Bar Graph

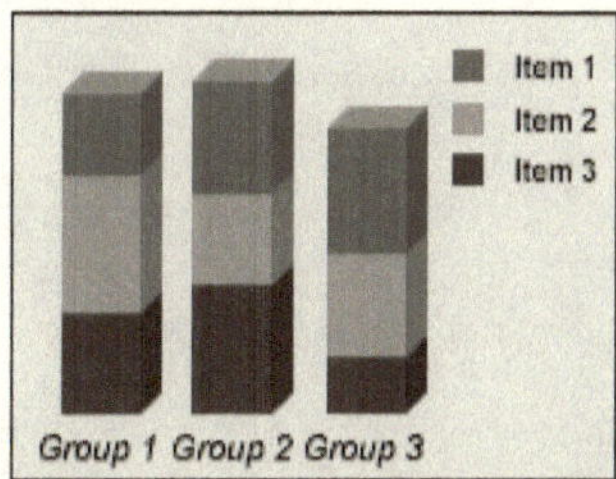

Stacked Vertical Bar Graph

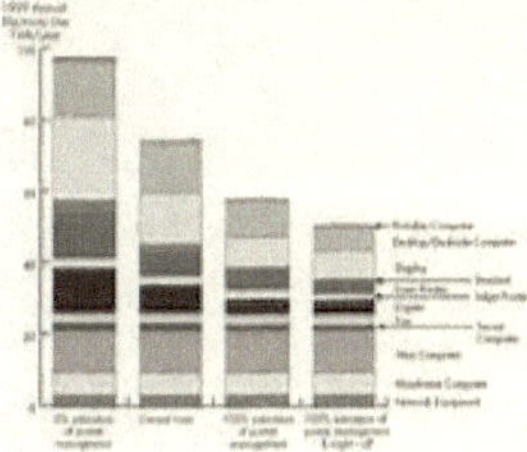

Stacked effect (blank spaces in bars)

Line Graph

A line graph is used to compare responses.

- ➤ Put time or levels on the horizontal axis (X-axis)
- ➤ Avoid more than 3 or 4 lines on a graph
- ➤ Connect points for continuous data to show a relationship
- ➤ Do not connect points for discrete data. If discrete dots obtained, it is better to use a bar chart and compare

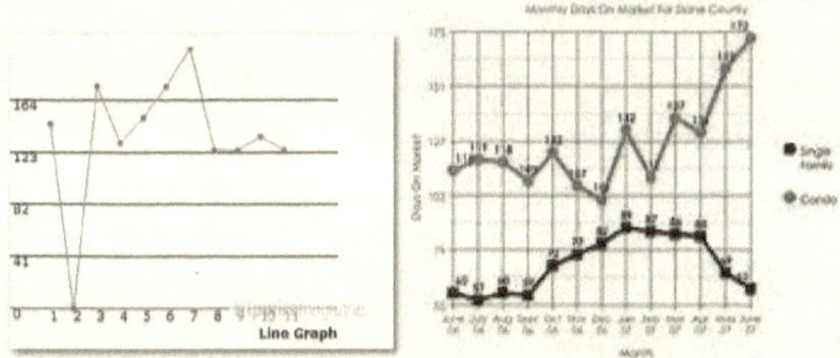

Scatter diagram

It is used to show correlation between two variables

- ➤ Use a mixed graph to show actual data and fitted (predicted) regression line (best fit line)

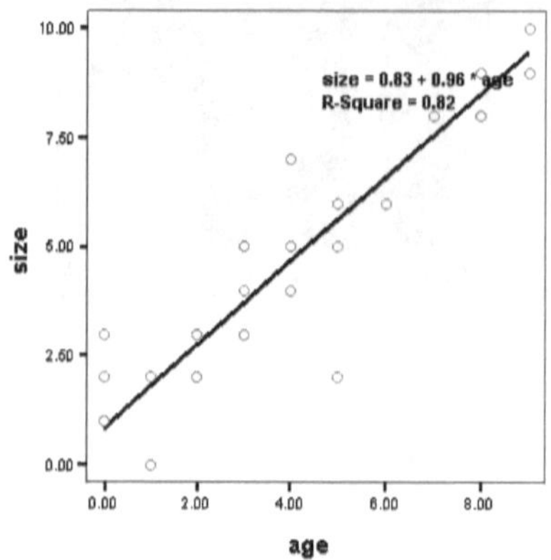

3.8.   Writing Numbers

In using numbers within a text,

- ➢ spell out « one » through « nine » (check Journal for information)
- ➢ use numerals
    - ▪ for numbers 10 and above
    - ▪ with a unit of measurement
        - • 5 kg, 20 days, 20 USD, 80%, 50°C
    - ▪ With a modifier
        - • Group 2, Eperiment 3, day 3, Equation 4.1 etc.
- ➢ Check Journal requirements for specifications in relation to commas in between numbers
    - ▪ 3,000 or 3000
- ➢ Be aware of differences in decimal points
    - ▪ US: 12,345.67
    - ▪ EU: 12.345.67
    - ▪ FR: 12 345.67
- ➢ If necessary, spell out numbers (and units) at the beginning of a sentence, but avoid using numbers at the start of a sentence if possible
    - ▪ Ten grams, **Not Ten g or 10g**.
- ➢ To indicate a range in numbers:
    - ▪ 30 to 60 inclusive (UK standards)
    - ▪ 30 through 60 (US standards)
    - ▪ **Not 30 – 60.**
- ➢ For a series where some numbers are fewer than 10 and others above ten, be consistent.
    - ▪ 2 X, 6 Y, 12 Z
    - ▪ **Not two X, six X and 12 Z**

- ➢ Use a word for a large number that ends with many zeros

    - ▪ 380 million (0.38 billion) people

    - ▪ Not 380,000,000 people

    - ▪ In tables and figures use:

        - • (in thousands), (in '000'), (in 10^3)

        - • Not $x10^3$ or 10^{-3}

- ➢ Be conscious that some numbers can be confused with some letters (depend on the font)

    - ▪ Number 1 and letter I

    - ▪ Number 0 and letter O

- ➢ Be conscious that some symbols can be confused with some letters

    - ▪ Multiplication sign x and letter x

    - ▪ Greek chi X, χ and letter x, x

3.9. Writing Dates

- ✦ Avoid writing dates only in numbers

    - ▪ Spell out the month

        US system: 02/10/01 ⟹ February 10, 2001 ⎫ interpreted differently in

        EU system: 02/10/01 ⟹ 2nd October, 2001 ⎬ numeric systems of

        CN system: 02/10/01 ⟹ 1st October, 2002 ⎭ different countries/continent

- ✦ Use three-letter abbreviations for months with long spellings (> 4 letters)

    - ▪ Jan., Feb., Mar., Apr., Aug., Sep., Oct., Nov., and Dec.,

- ✦ Spell out months with three or four letters

    - ▪ May, June, and July

3.10 Writing Time

- ✦ Use a 24-hour clock to express time (a.m. – p.m. system)

    - ▪ 0:00 (midnight), 010:20; 12:00 (noon)

    - ▪ Not 12:00 a.m. or 12:00 p.m. but 12 noon, 12 midday, midnight

- ✦ Express length of time in hours and minutes

    - ▪ 3 H 15 min. not 3:15 time of the day

- ✦ Abbreviate units of time when used with a number

    - ▪ Year(s) = yr(s) 3yrs

    - ▪ Month(s) = mon.

    - ▪ Week(s) = wk

    - ▪ Day(s) = d

    - ▪ Hour(s) = h

- Minute(s) = min
- Second(s) = s

End of 2015

3.11   Publishing Process

Preparing Paper for Publishing

- Choice of Journal

    - Mission

    - Audience

    - Visibility

    - Impact factor (measure of quality and quantity)

- Contact editor for information

    - Send abstract, if in doubt

- Instructions for authors

    - Download from Journal's website

- Read and follow instructions

    - Margins, spacing, line numbers, headings, references, maximum key strokes (max ks), tables, figures, keywords, running head etc.

- Instructions vary per type of paper

    - Research article, review articles, special topics, technical notes, letters to the editor

- Spell check and proof read before submission.

Submission of Manuscript

- Read and follow instructions carefully
- Two forms of submission

    - Direct electronic submission

        - Check URL

    - Proxy electronic submission

        - Paper and disk

        - Check address

        - Expect delays

- Submit "cover" letter stating objectives of the research

Submission Forms

Fill out the following forms:

- Manuscript submission form
    - Assures that paper is not submitted somewhere else
    - Assures that each author reads paper
    - Ensures "sign off" on the paper by reviewers.
        - Difficult in International publishing: each reviewer signs off on his/her copy and send to the author(s).
- Copyright release form
    - Available online or in journal
    - Releases copyright to journal
    - If permission for copyright (©) material is needed, then show source of material

Referees

- Journal Chooses referees
    - Society members
    - Reference list (within or outside society by subject topic)
    - Experience of section editors
- Author's suggestion
    - At most 04 persons desired (avoid naming friends)
    - At most 04 undesired persons
- Usually editor plus 02 referees (01 from author's list, 01 from Journal's list)

Submitted Paper Review

- Timely and confidential
    - Unbiased
    - Constructive
        - Provide help for members
- Recommendations from:
    - Reviewers
    - Section editors
    - Editor-in-chief
        - Final decision

Decisions

Decisions could be:

- Accepted
    - Accepted with no change

- Accepted with minor changes
        - Accepted with majour changes
- Rejected reasons
    - Does not meet the standards of the Journal
        - Incomplete work
        - Evidence does not support conclusion
        - Poorly conceived research design. etc.
    - Better suited for another Journal
    - Does not add new knowledge

- What to do if paper is rejected
    - Discuss with the section editor
    - Appeal to the editor-in-chief
        - If judgement is wrong or unfair
    - Resubmit to another section, if advised to do so
    - Resubmit to another Journal
        - Revise according to the review comments
- Causes for revision
    - Did not follow style and format
    - Incomplete statistical analysis
    - Lack of clarity or brevity
    - Issues related to facts or theory
    - Poor organization of tables and figures
    - Grammatical errors
    - Etc.

- Responding to Reviewers
    - Receive acceptance letter from editor-in-chief
    - Do not be angry for comments
    - Consider comments seriously
        - Read carefully to be sure that they are well understood
    - Revise or defend yourself
        " I have revised the paper as suggested by reviewers, except for…."
- Proof read revisions carefully
    - Make corrections on a copy

- Use standard proof marks
  - Rewrite extensive changes
  - Last chance to fix errors and layout
- Return edited work quickly (within 3 days)
  - Fax with approval form
  - Use electronic "return receipt" (can verify when reviewers received paper)
- Publication charges
  - Check if pages are charged
    - commercial Journals,
    - society journals (members vs nonmembers)
  - Who pays the page charges? (decide early on)
  - Is there an extra charge for colour prints
  - Is there a possibility to order reprints
    - Minimum: 50 to 100 copies

Ethics in scientific publication: Authorship and Ownership of Data

It is wrong to:

- Fabricate data (making up results, creating data points that make the results look good)
- Falsify data (temper with results e.g. eliminating data points that do not look right)
- Plagiarise (steal somebody's ideas or data)

Ethical issues to be careful about

- Duplicating publication
- Conflicts of interests in discussing results
- Publishing sensitive material
- Publishing unethical research
- Ownership of data
- Authorship of data

Authorship

- Who is an author? In what order?
  - Persons who have highly contributed intellectually to the paper to take public responsibility. The following conditions should be met:
    - Conception, design or analysis and interpretation of data
    - Drafting the paper or reviewing it critically for important intellectual content
    - Final approval of the version to be published
    - Ordering starts with main author (greatest contribution)

- Acknowledge those who have made small contributions to the paper
- Attributing credit for published papers varies according to the country
- Credit for published papers are shared among all authors
- All authors share joint responsibility (especially when there is a screw up)

Ownership of data

This issue is resolved by answering the following questions:

- Who collected the data?
- Under whose intellectual direction and guidance were the data collected?
- Were the rights to the data assigned?
- Can part of the original data be used to prepare a report or manuscript?
- Should anyone be allowed access to data?

In general, intellectual property right belongs to the University and the Student

Chapter 4: Research Methodology: Scientific Techniques for Writing Theses and Term Papers

The teaching/learning method for this topic will include:

- **Lectures and group discussions/exercises**

- **Analysis of Sample Research Proposals (Projects) that will be evaluated at the end of the course. These could be group of individual proposals**

  - ➢ **Presentations of the group/individual Research proposals will be considered as your mid- term exam**

  - ➢ **The group/individual research proposals (project) will be considered as the final exams**

Elaboration of the group research proposal (project) will start from the beginning of this section and should follow the different steps in the course

Group or Individual Research Proposal

Imagine that you are writing your thesis or research proposal as a group or an individual.

(Form working groups of your choice based on your study program).

Each group/individual should choose one area of study/specialisation from the list below and develop the different aspects of the research proposal based on the discussions of each class.

Each aspect (facet) of the research proposal developed based on the discussions of the previous class shall be presented during the next class for correction.

International Development Students

- Program and Project Management for Sustainable Development
- Advanced Gender Studies and Issues for Sustainable Development in Africa
- Community Development Practice and International Development
- The Challenge of HIV/AIDS, Roll Back Malaria Initiative for Africa   and Other
- Environmental Conservation, Natural Resources and Sustainable Development
- Resources Mobilization, Grants Writing, Networking /Building Partnerships in Development Epidemics in Sustainable Development
- Food Technologies, Appropriate Technologies and Sustainable Livelihoods in Development Practice
- Conflict Prevention Strategies, Management and Peace Building for Development
- Environmental Conservation and Climate Change Issues In Development
- Research Design And Methodology for Social Sciences
- Advanced Transformation Management
- Millennium Development Goals, European Consensus 2005 – European Union-ACP Development Policy

4.   Research Proposal Writing

The discussions in this section present a model outline for developing a research proposal for the thesis that can be used as a point of departure for discussion with supervisors. This outline varies according to the expectations of supervisors, defence committee (in the case of the total involvement approach), funding agency or University/Department. However, the variation is not so great.

4.1. Definition of research

It refers to a systematic investigation whose purpose is to acquire new information and knowledge, facts, appropriate solutions to an identified problem in a specific area, and deduce theory and make generalisations.

4.2. Definition of research proposal

It is a scholarly (orderly and thorough) document that sets the minimum core intellectual contribution of one's thesis to the existing body of knowledge in a specific field (area of study).

It refers to what the researcher proposes or intends to do in the thesis writing process.

It is a document that specifies:

- what the researcher intends to do,

- what are the criteria for ensuring what has to be done,

- why carry out the research in a particular area,

- what is expected to be achieved by carrying out the research (significance or knowledge gap to be filled),

- How it will be done and how the results will be interpreted (methodology).

It contains all the key elements involved in the research process and the necessary information that guides the evaluation of the proposed study or area of research.

It is a general plan, scheme, structure and strategy that are designed to obtain (acquire) answers to specific research questions that are raised in a research project.

It is also called a research protocol or "avant-projet de recherché in French".

It is a detailed operational plan for obtaining answers to questions raised in a research project.

4.3. Purpose of elaborating a research proposal

- ➢ To provide sufficient information that convinces readers (supervisor(s), committee, etc.) that the researcher has:

- an important idea that needs investigation;

- a good mastery of the relevant literature and the majour issues to the idea to be investigated;

- a sound methodology for the research

- The competence to work and elaborate a work plan that permits the completion of a research project.

➢ To provide a document that serves as a contract between the supervisor(s), committee (in case of total involvement) and the candidate (student, researcher).

- By approving the proposal, the supervisor(s) or committee judge that the research approach is reasonable and is most likely to produce the expected results;

- An implicit agreement of supervisor(s)/committee acceptance of the research results as being adequate for the purpose of obtaining/granting a degree.

➢ To show that the researcher (student) is:

- engaging in a genuine enquiry (finding out about something worthwhile in a specific context);

- able to link up his/her proposed work with the work of other scholars (relevant schools of thought in the topic area);

- able to establish a scientific orientation and a methodological approach;

- able to give consideration for ethical issues related to the research.

➢ It helps in estimating the size of the research project.

NB1: the quality of a research proposal depends on the quality of the proposed project and the actual proposal writing.

The researcher's writing (manner of presenting the ideas and steps) should be coherent, clear and convincing (captivating).

NB2: A poorly written research proposal may lead to the rejection of a good research project.

4.4. Length of a research proposal

An ideal research proposal should be concise and its length should range between 05 to 15 pages. It could be longer according to the topic and ideas discussed (existing body of knowledge).

4.5. Structure

The structure of a research proposal (protocol; "avant-projet de recherché") is determined by the kind of research to be carried out:

- primary research

- secondary research

4.5.1. Secondary research (desk top research):

- gathering data from existing data that has been collected and analysed by some other person;

- a detailed methodology or research methods may not be very necessary;

- requires an outline specifying the approach to answering the research problem, the theoretical framework, the area of research, issues or authors of relevant literature;

- requires specifying primary sources of data collection such as original texts/literature, films, magazines, novels, poems, original records, reports, letters, journals, diaries, museums;

Illustrates who and what to use to access data, why and how relevant is the data in answering the research question.

4.5.2. Primary Research (empirical research)

Collecting data using different methods of data collection and analysis (experiments, interviews [structured, semi-structured, unstructured], surveys, statistical charts)

A detailed research proposal is needed

Include a research design, variables and indicators and methodology

4.5.3 Research Proposal Outline

Title

Preliminaries (table of content, acronyms, etc.)

Abstract

Introduction

Topic of discussion (area of focus or discussion) or main idea or justification

Objective(s)

Main objective

Specific objectives

Background (rationale, context and justification)

Literature Review and theoretical or conceptual perspective

Concepts to be used in the research

Implications of the research or thesis

The Research Problem (problem statement)

Research Questions

Main research question

Sub research questions

Hypotheses

a. Main hypothesis

b. Sub hypotheses

Methodology

Expected Results

Chronogram

Research Budget

Bibliography or References

Title (working title)

It should catch the reader's interest and be inclined (prompted) to the proposal content;

It should be clear, concise and descriptive and reflect the likely position of the researcher;

Often stated in terms of a functional relationship

Indicates the independent and dependent variables

It should be informative and catchy

Not more than seven words

Example

Proper recruitment as a pre-condition for a profitable business enterprise within the Beta firm of Austin, Texas.

A review of the science base to support the development of health warnings for tobacco packages

Economic and environmental assessment of irrigation water policies: A bio economic simulation study

Impact of Development Aid in Canada. The case of the Toronto's Highway

Framers and Ambivalence in Context: An Analysis of Hands-On Experts' Perception of the Welfare of Animals in Traveling Circuses in The Netherlands

Agricultural policy and the Dutch agricultural institutional matrix during the transition from organized to disorganized capitalism

Agricultural Policy and Food Security in the U.S.A : The Case of Cotton Farmers in Maryland

Germano-French Cooperation and the Decentralization Program: The Support Program for Decentralization and Local Development (PADDL) in the Mbalmayo Municipality.

3.5.3.2.   Abstract

It is a brief summary of the work (research) that has to be done.

It should include:

The key points what, why, how and where of the research;

The research question, hypothesis, background and implication of the study;

A brief description of the objective of the study, the research population, methods (design, procedures, sample and instruments), expected results (the main findings) and a time frame;

A definition of the central hypothesis, description of the site and population to be studied;

A summary of the total time necessary to carry out the research (if necessary);

It should have no abbreviations;

key words (not more than 05)

It should be written in one paragraph only

It should not be longer than 200 to 300 words

NB: It is the last thing to be written even though it is part of the preliminaries!!!

Example of an abstract

Abstract

SHARP (a Structured, Holistic Approach for a Research Proposal) is a structured method for developing a research proposal that can be used either by individuals or by teams of researchers. The eight steps in SHARP are (1) setting up a causal model, (2) establishing a fact-hypothesis matrix (FaHM), (3) developing a variable-indicator-method matrix (VIM), (4) selecting the study design, (5) defining the sampling procedure and calculating the sample size, (6) selecting the statistical methods, (7) considering the ethical aspects, and (8) setting up an operational plan. The objectives of the research proposal are to help the researcher to define the contents and to plan and execute a research project, and to inform potential collaborators and supporters about the topic. The proposal that is produced during the process can be submitted to agencies for possible funding.

Key words: SHARP, method, research proposal, eight steps, objectives

Exercise: Group work (15 minutes)

Each group should analyze the research abstracts that have been given to them:

i)   Verify whether the title is correctly written

ii) **Evaluate wither the abstract follows the structure and content of the research proposal abstract discussed above;**

ii) **Propose necessary amendments if any.**

3.5.3.3.   Introduction to the research proposal

It is an interesting and informative opening paragraph(s) to the research proposal:

a brief overview that tells the reader what the research proposal is all about;

it highlights the need for further research;

it includes:

i) a research topic of discussion or area of focus of discussion or justification, and

ii) research objectives.

Research Topic of discussion or area of focus of discussion or justification for the research or arguments

Research topic or area of discussion selection is a majour hindrance to thesis write-up for students.

Definition:

A thesis or research topic (area of focus, justification) is a subject of research (analysis, discussion and conclusion) that provides information to the reader what the thesis is all about.

a brief overview that tells a well-informed or non-specialist reader what the scholar (student, candidate, researcher etc.) wants to research on and present in his/her thesis;

a general field of consideration from which arguments can be drawn in a research or thesis.

also called the area of focus or justification for the research or thesis.

It is not a title of a thesis, but highlights and explains the type of information that can help in an understanding of the title.

developed based on previous scientific discourse or existing shared knowledge.

announces the main theme of the research;

should be clearly written and should let others assess the relevance of the research to them so as to attract their interest;

should not be too broad or too narrow in scope.

Should not be short nor too long:

Usually one paragraph but not longer than a page but can go beyond if absolutely necessary;

consists of a **topic sentence** and relevant scientific issues of discussion in relation to the topic sentence.

Topic Sentence

It is usually the 1st sentence in the first paragraph of the research area of focus or topic or justification, around which ideas or arguments are developed.

A topic sentence is the most important sentence in a paragraph.

It helps organize the paragraph by summarizing the information in that paragraph.

It should put forward an argument and use some words from the title

It is a sentence or statement that orients the scientific discussion of the proposal.

Purpose of the Thesis Topic Sentence

It suggests or states the main idea (topic) of discussion in the thesis;

It tells what the rest of the paragraph is about;

It is like a road map that will tell the reader or listener to understand the researcher's view point;

It should be:

concise and emphatic (ideas /words placed in key positions in a text to give them special weight and prominence);

clear and strong;

It often uses phrases such as:

One of the main reasons for …..

One of the major factors in ………… is…………….

Generally speaking, ………

One of the strongest arguments against/ in favour of………is ….

One of the main advantages / disadvantages of …………,is ……

It has a **topic** and a **controlling idea**. The controlling idea shows the direction of the paragraph. Think of an **idea (topic)** and what you want to say about the **idea (controlling factor).**

Examples of a research/thesis topic sentence

There are many possible contributing factors to global warming.

The topic is "global warming"

the controlling factor is "many possible contributing factors."

Teenage pregnancy may be prevented through improved education.

The topic is "teenage pregnancy prevention"

the controlling idea is "improved education."

There are many reasons why pollution in Yaounde Town is the worst in the world.

The topic is "pollution in Yaounde Town is the worst in the world" and the controlling idea is "many reasons."

Exercise: Brainstorm on topic sentences that are related to your area of focus for your research.

Example of a research topic/area of focus or justification

One of the strongest arguments in favour of a relaxed approach to immigration is that the UK benefits economically from immigrant labour. Research shows that countries with high levels of immigration are economically successful and that there is a correlation between a mobile labour force and economic prosperity (quote author, year of publication). Immigration serves as an important source of both skilled and unskilled labour in the UK which has come to depend on migrants to plug gaps in its skilled professions and to do jobs that the local population are unwilling to do.

Online learning has its problems. Although student surveys always show that students like to have access to materials online, the take up of purely online courses is low. When questioned, students find that studying online can be a lonely and unsatisfying experience. Not only do students miss the human interaction with other students, they also find the time lag in getting answers to their questions very frustrating.

One of the most important factors leading to the outbreak of World War One was the arms race between Britain and Germany. Britain had an empire at this time and Germany wanted a similar role in the world. This meant having a strong navy so the Germans spent a considerable amount of time and effort building up its naval force. Britain responded to this threat to its dominance by strengthening its navy even further. This 'naval race' contributed to the increase in tension between the two countries.

Margaret Thatcher's policies were dominated by the philosophy of individual freedom and self-reliance. During the years of the Thatcher government, Britons experienced cuts in welfare payments and drastic legal restrictions on trade unions. Public industries were sold off to private investors in the belief that the free market would deliver prosperity to all.

Selecting and developing a thesis topic or focus area or justification can be based on the following:

1. Knowledge and experience in the specific area;

2. Desire for Career Advancement

3. Acceptability to Supervisor(s)

4. Recommendations for further study from other thesis

5. Current Career Orientations or work

Once a topic area is identified, elaborate a statement and do a literature search and expand on it.

Once a thesis topic is selected, delimitation of its scope should be based on three criteria:

a. Possibility of Access to Data

b. Time allocated for data collection

c. budget

Guiding questions to the choice of thesis topic

Once a thesis topic is selected, use the following questions to verify the ideas before defining and developing the topic:

HOW?   How does the topic fit with respect to the field (where the data will be collected)?

WHERE?   Where does the topic take place geographically or culturally?

WHEN?   When did the topic become important or of issue?

WHO?   Who are the people involved or affected?

WHY?   Why is the topic important?

WHAT?   What makes the research unique?

NB: In elaborating a topic area, coherence and scientific orientations should be the guiding principle:

- no two ideas discussed in a paragraph;

- present and discuss ideas and paragraphs in a chronological order: do not jump to another idea when paragraphs concerning a specific idea are not yet exhausted;

- it should be based on the scientific orientation in that area, and the new idea that one's research is intended to contribute to the scientific debate around this topic;

- in-text citation of other scholars works in the same area of focus should be included whenever their ideas are mentioned;

- it should demonstrate the ability of the researcher to make use of other scholars' work in his/her own intentions/work.

i) Research Objectives

Research objectives are the stated intentions of the achievements to be attained by carrying out the research.

They are set based on the need to answer the question "why carry out the research".

They are set in relation to the purpose or aim of the research

Two aspects:

- Main (Global, General) research objective

- Specific objectives

a) Main Objective

It is defined as the purpose of the research.

It states what the project intends to accomplish or develop in relation to observed problems or situations.

Criteria for formulating a main (global, general) research objective

An objective must be:

- applicable to the situation;

- Achievable, measurable and time bound (principle of SMART);

- not be ambiguous;

- harmonious with societal and institutional goals and constraints;

- **Begins with "To"**

Example

To assess whether all staff of the Moon Bank have an equal chance of finding out about its forthcoming promotion opportunities which maybe a hindrance to their professional development.

To increase the profitability of the Fokou business enterprise in Yaounde within 05 years through the use of proper recruitment strategies

To document the relationship between foreign aid and social, economic and infrastructural development as a measure of attaining the social wellbeing of Cameroonians from 2000 to 2015

Class Exercise: Brainstorm on possible main objectives to your research

Specific research objectives

These are component research objectives (a breakdown of the general research objective)

They state specific research results and sequential goals to be achieved during the study.

They are concrete, attainable results that can be measured and are readily identified when they have been reached.

They must be necessary *and* sufficient to reach the general objective of the research project.

For a Master thesis, 02 to 03 specific objectives are enough to facilitate comprehension and reduce the amount of work involved in the research.

Example:

To evaluate the formal and informal processes of promotion within the Moon Bank

To identify the different levels of access to information for all staff of the Moon Bank

To document the relationship between promotion processes, staff access to information and professional development within the Moon Bank

 To investigate the type of foreign aid that Cameroon has received between 2000 and 2014

To identify the types of social, economic and infrastructural development that has occurred between 2000 and 2014 in Cameroon

To relate foreign aid, the different types of development and human welfare (wellbeing) and make possible recommendations for improvement in Cameroon

Class exercise: group work (20 minutes)
You have been given some research proposal introductions. Read through them and evaluate in terms of:

- The quality of the topic area with respect to its structure, content including logical and scientific arguments made
- Evaluate the type of in-text citation
- Propose recommendations for improvement.

Assignment 2

Based on the groups formed (or individually) and the area of study/specialisation chosen, elaborate:

i. a research proposal title

ii. an introduction to the proposal that should include

    a. a focus area: a topic sentence, other arguments

    b. research objectives (main objective, specific objectives)

    c. in-text citation

3. Background (context of the research)

It addresses the historical, cultural, political, social, economic, environmental, organisational and current state of information about the context of the research or area of interest;

- It may include a theoretical starting point, personal motivation and policy (policies).
- It reveals what problem the research is attempting to address within a specific context
- It states clearly why there is a problem that needs to be addressed
  - What knowledge gap is there that needs to be filled
    - Knowledge not mentioned in existing literature in the field of study

- It highlights the need to apply certain ideas in a specific context

  02 main issues are:

  - how the research came to being (genesis or origin of the idea being researched),
  - the relationship of the topic of research to other research in the field of study

- It specifies who is undertaking the research and for whom, where the research is to be carried out and who are the subjects of research.

Purpose:

To situate the reader or researcher in the context in which the research is being carried out

Example

The case of the Impact of Development aid in Cameroon: The case of the Yaounde – Douala Highway

Type of background information needed:

- **Historical perspective of development aid in general and Cameroon in particular;**
- **The impact of various types of development aid in other parts of the world and Cameroon**
- **Culture of the people living along the Yaounde Douala Highway (project affected area);**
- **Demography of the people living along the Yaounde-Douala Highway;**
- **Climatic factors**
- **Topography**
- **Vegetation**
- **Soil types**
- **Crops and livestock**
- **Forms of Livelihoods**
- **etc**

Exercise: group work

In your respective groups, read through the thesis background that you have been given and evaluate it in terms of:

- its content
- whether it is clear and understandable (does it situate the reader to the context of the research)
- highlight what is lacking and propose necessary improvements

4. **Literature review and theoretical perspective or conceptual framework**

- These specify the state of the scientific knowledge that exists in the area of focus or study

- They help the researcher to identify knowledge gaps (what has not been said by other scholars) in the area of focus (topic of the research)

- The relevant variables and concepts are defined and discussed in this section.

- This section provides the theoretical or conceptual basis for the research and it should not be exhaustive

- Specify concepts, paradigm (perspective, orientation) and theoretical assumptions the researcher is making or questioning

- Discussions in this section should be well structured and organised to permit the flow of ideas
  - focused, united and coherent
  - not repetitive
  - should not depend too much on secondary sources of information/knowledge
  - cite influential literature and not irrelevant and trivial ones
  - should be shaped by the researcher's arguments and seek to establish a theoretical or conceptual orientation
- Discussions should be based on current literature (keep up with recent developments);
  - Literature above 10 years old to the period of the research and thesis writing is not always advisable, except otherwise (in a situation where a specific issue has not been discussed in the recent literature)

- Literature review and theoretical or conceptual perspective should be related to the:
  - Research topic
  - Research methods (justifications for the use of a particular methodology for the research)
  - Research data to be collected
  - Research expected outcome (results), recommendations, and conclusions (if possible)
- Discussions should start with the more general studies and end up with more focused studies that are relevant to the research topic.

Importance

- ensures that the researcher is not inventing something;
- gives credit to scholars who have provided the basis for researching a specific topic (scientific area of focus);
- demonstrates the researcher's knowledge of the problem to be researched;
- demonstrates the researcher's understanding of the theoretical and conceptual issues related to the research topic;
- reveals the researcher's ability to critically evaluate, integrate and synthesize existing literature that is relevant to the research focus (topic);
- highlights new theoretical insights and the possibilities of developing models for the conceptual framework for the research;
- convinces the reader that the research will make useful, significant and reasonable contributions to the existing knowledge base in the study area

- Help resolve an important theoretical issue
- Help fill a majour knowledge gap in the literature.

Theoretical perspective or conceptual framework:

- It is a combination of factors that a researcher is focusing on in his/her research;

- It is a hypothetical model that provides explanations for a given point in view;

- Its development involves focusing on important variables in the study and making connections among them. A variable could also be called a factor(s) that determines or influences the topic of discussion.

- Making connections and discussing relationships among these factors while using existing literature and the researcher's arguments constitute a theoretical or conceptual framework.

In elaborating a theoretical or conceptual framework (perspective):

- Each idea or fact related to a specific variable or concept or theory should be discussed per paragraph;
- Each idea could have more than one literature citation, which should all be put in the same paragraph.
- Discuss one variable or concept at a time and then link it up to another before starting its discussion.

NB: Literature review could either be a standalone section or incorporated into either the theoretical or conceptual framework.

How to write a literature review if it is a standalone section

- It should classify and evaluate the themes of the texts that are relevant to the research;
- It should have an introduction, body of the text, and conclusion.

Introduction Includes:

- The nature of the topic of the research
- Parameters of the topic (what it includes and excludes)
- The basis for selecting the literature

The body should include texts in relation to:

- Theoretical, conceptual or ideological viewpoints (current mainstream versus alternative issues);
    - Differing theoretical assumptions
    - Differing political outlooks (if applicable)
    - Other conflicting ideologies
- Approaches used (empirical, desktop [secondary research], philosophical, historical, postmodernist etc.);
- Definitions of concepts used and their interrelations[1];
- Current research studies and discoveries in the area of focus or research topic;
- Principal questions of clarification that are being asked;
- General conclusions that are being drawn by other scholars in relation to the topic;
- The methodologies and methods used.

Conclusion should include:

- A summary of majour agreements and disagreements in the literature read;
- A summary of the general conclusions that are being drawn by other scholars in relation to the topic;
- A summary of where one's thesis is placed in the literature.

NB: Samples of literature reviews are given to students for analysis and recommendations

5. **Implications of the research or thesis**
    - It refers to an indication of the significance of the study (research) and the ways in which the research results will advance an understanding of the issues under discussion.

This relates to:

- the importance of the research (what are the intensions of carrying out the research)
- what are the benefits of doing the research
- in what ways or how will the research results contribute to the existing body of knowledge in the field of study.

Example:

---

[1] Author, year, title, website, date downloaded

Commercial benefits, changes in current practices, a new perspective or orientation on an old issue or topic of debate, benefits to the community and scientific community and knowledge, a pre-requisite for obtaining the required degree etc.

6   The Research Problem or problem statement

A research **problem** is a concise description of the issue(s) that need to be addressed by the researcher.

The reader must be able to discern the seriousness of the problem and understand the need for the study and its further elucidation. Therefore, citations are needed in this section.

In this section, one seeks to:

- Present the knowledge gap(s) that needs to be researched and filled thus situating one's work in the scientific debate;
- State the existing problem that arises as a result of the knowledge gap;
- State the consequences of the existing problem;
- State the desired situation

It refers to giving a vivid description of the problem as perceived by the researcher.

The research problem has three parts

- Ideal situation
- Reality (real situation)
  - Here, specify what areas of enquiry will be needed to arrive at the ideal situation.
- Consequences of the problem if no solution is sort (this highlights the benefits of the research).

The research problem should be clear and well-articulated.

It should clearly describe the nature and extent of the problem that the study wants to solve.

It emanates from the research topic and the background to the research that is developed in the introductory part of the research proposal (protocol).

It should clearly state what are the scope and limitations (in time, money, resources, technologies) that can be used to solve the problem?

It should clearly identify and represent the variables (factors) that contribute to the problem and therefore should be studied.

It should highlight the direct and indirect impact of the problem to be studied.

It sets the stage for the definition of research questions and hypotheses.

It helps the reader anticipate the goal of each study or research.

Steps in developing the research problem

1. **Set up a topic statement**. The topic statement, or opening statement, will identify the problem, and is an important part of the research problem.

2. **Identify various solutions** to the problem. The placement of these solutions depends on the overall format of the research problem, but generally, these are presented in the context of fact after the problem has been clearly identified.

3. **Apply the 5 W's**. Within the research problem, keep the focus on presenting a diversity of facts as possible. This includes common words such as: who, what, why, when, where and how. Addressing each of these can make a problem statement more informative and effective.

4. **Think about including a vision in the research problem**. The vision for a research problem is simply described as "what you want" or what the group wants out of the situation. In other words, it is the desirable outcome.

5. **Conclude the research problem**. Bring all of these information together in an effective conclusion that restates the issue and the main ideas that the researcher is trying to address.

Example of a research problem 1

Overfill has been a serious problem facing our city waste facilities for the last decade. By some estimation, our city dumps are on average 30% above capacity—an unsanitary, unsafe, and unwise position for our city to be in.

Several methods have been proposed in order to combat this. Perhaps the most popular of these is the simplest: building two new landfills on the county's outskirts. Others have proposed stronger recycling campaigns and larger per-bag waste disposal costs as a way to lessen the potential damage of our trash situation.

Bluffington is close to drowning in trash. Action is needed if our city is to remain the clean safe place to live that it has always been.

Example of a research problem 2

"Essay mills"—companies that sell pre-written and/or custom works for students to purchase and turn in as their own work—have been an increasing problem for universities across the nation since the advent of the Internet. Some researchers believe that over 10% of papers turned in come from one of these services (or from similar plagiarism, like buying from friends).

In order to combat this, stronger analytical tools are needed to compare the student's past body of work to the existing work being turned in. Professors, overworked as they can be, need also turn a sharper eye toward the work they're given.

Students turning in work improperly labeled as their own are a serious problem to every school that wants to be taken seriously. We must take more steps in analyzing the work to mitigate the practice's impact on education and society.

Example 3

With the national trend toward more patient care in outpatient settings, the number of patients on in-patient wards has declined in many hospitals, contributing to the inadequacy of inpatient wards as the primary setting for teaching students.

Medical students are therefore mostly undergoing classroom training and only few practical sessions done which leads to poorly trained personnel.

The consequences of poor training leads to improper health care services rendered to patients and increased death rates in some cases.

Class exercise: Students read through the problem statements of past students' theses and criticise.

8   Research Question

It refers to what you intend to research (variables, place, subjects)

Two aspects:

- o Main research question
- o Sub research questions

a) Main research question

It refers to the global idea of what is intended to be researched

Example:

What factors contribute to employees' belief that they are being discriminated against by their immediate supervisors in cross-gender and cross-cultural supervisor-employee relationships which have led to employee dissatisfaction within the Guiness - Cameroon Company in Yaounde?

b) Sub research questions

These are a breakdown of the main research question into smaller and simpler questions according to the different variables contained in the main research question.

Example:

Sub question 1: What factors lead to supervisor(s) discrimination against employees in the Yaounde Guiness – Cameroon Company branch?

Or

Are employees of Guiness Cameroon Yaounde branch being discriminated upon by their supervisors?

Or

In what ways are the employees of Guiness Cameroon Yaounde branch being discriminated upon by their supervisors?

Sub question 2: What type of cross-gender and cross-cultural supervisor – employee relationships exist within the Guiness Cameroon Yaounde branch?

Or

Are there cross-gender and cross-cultural supervisor – employee relations existing within Guiness Cameroon Yaounde branch?

Sub question 3: How can employee satisfaction be improved in cross-cultural and cross-gender supervisor-employee relationships within the Guiness Cameroon Yaounde branch?

Class exercise: Brainstorming on possible research questions for students' research topics

9   Hypotheses

A hypothesis is a testable statement about the expected relationship between two or more variables.

It is a reconversion of the research question into a statement that can be tested through data gathering and either correlational analysis or causal connections to see whether it is supported or not.

A hypothesis should be:

» based on a known fact or theory;

» testable;

» specific;

» brief, but clear.

Two types of hypotheses: a main hypothesis and sub hypotheses.

a) Main hypothesis

Example:

Within the Yaounde branch of the Guiness Cameroon company, many factors lead to supervisors' discrimination against employees in cross-gender and cross-cultural supervisor-employee relationships which have led to employee dissatisfaction and therefore their low or poor perfomance.

Or

The rate (level) of employee dissatisfaction within the Guiness Cameroon Yaounde branch is high due to the existence of discriminatory cross-gender and cross-cultural supervisor-employee relationships that have led to their low performance.

b)   Sub hypotheses

These state relationships between variables that are part of, or complement, the interpretation of the main hypothesis

It is a breakdown or components that permit the measuring of the main hypothesis.

Sub hypothesis 1:
The more the employee perceives the supervisor as performing the mentoring role, the less the employee will feel discriminated against by the supervisor.

Sub hypothesis 2
The less the scornful and derogatory way in which supervisors give performance feedback to employees, the less employees will feel discriminated against by the supervisor in cross-gender and cross-cultural supervisor – employee relationships within the Guiness Cameroon Yaounde branch

Or

The lower the level of mutual trust that exists between the employee and the supervisor, the more the employee feels discriminated upon in cross-cultural and cross-gender supervisor-employee relationships within the Guiness Cameroon Yaounde branch

Sub hypothesis 3: Employee satisfaction in cross-cultural and cross-gender supervisor-employee relationships within the Guiness Cameroon Yaounde branch can be improved by setting control mechanisms that check against the discriminatory practices by supervisors.

Or

Discriminatory cross-gender and cross-cultural supervisor – employee relationships within the Guiness Cameroon Yaounde branch hinders personnel satisfaction.

Assignment 03:

10   Methodology

A methodology is a step-by-step presentation of the way in which the researcher plans or intends to carry out the research.

It specifies the specific methods and techniques that will be used for data collection and analysis. It deals with the practical aspects of what, who, how and where.

It seeks to address the following issues:
- How the study will be done;
- What the sources of data are;
- What type of data will be collected;

- What kinds of methods, procedures and instruments will be used for site selection, choosing the research subjects, data collection and analysis;
- Who should be included in the sample population and why;
- Ensuring reliability and validity of the results;
- The context in which the results will be interpreted, concluded and understood.

The elements that appear in the methodology section include:

a) Study site

b) Variables and indicators

c) Research design

d) Sampling (selection criteria, size and sample population, sub samples etc.)

e) Research Methods:

    ⬇ Data collection methods and their measurements

    i)   What methods will be used to collect the necessary data in the field

    ii)   What are their (definitions)

    iii)   Why is the method useful for the particular research

    iv)   How will these methods be applied to collect the data in the field

    ⬇ Data analysis methods

    i)   What are the methods to be used in analysing the data collected

        - Statistical analysis (test-statistics) to be used and their measurements (t-test, χ^2, F-test, R^2 etc)
            - What is it
            - Why choice of method for the analysis
            - How to apply the method to analyse the data

        - Qualitative analysis methods
            - What is it
            - Why choice of method for the analysis
            - How to apply the method to analyse the data

f) Interpretation and presentation of results

    - Graphics
    - Text
    - Tables
    - etc.

a. Study Site

This refers to a brief description of where the research will be carried out.

➢ Why choice

➢ Presentation of the site (population, characteristics, livelihood activities etc.)

➢ **Site Selection**

    o In this section, the criteria for the choice of the study site are explained.

e.g. ease of accessibility, financial constraints, intensive production activities etc.

b. Variables and indicators

Variable

It is a characteristic of the research subjects that has to be measured

e.g. nutritional status

A variable takes on many forms or characteristics or attributes

Exercise: brainstorm on some variables for students' research topics

Indicator (measurement)

It is a measurement that is collected during the research that is supposed to reflect the variable being measured.

It defines the variable exactly.

It is a translation of abstract concepts into observable behaviour that can be measured (case of behavioural research).

e.g. indicator for nutritional status will be: body mass index, body weight, height for age, weight for age etc.

e.g. indicator for development: social, economic, political environmental, cultural, spiritual development

social development: infrastructure: schools, road network, hospitals and health centres/units etc

Criteria for choice of an indicator:

➢ Validity: Does the instrument and indicator actually measure (quantify or describe) what is supposed to be measured (variable)?

➢ **Feasibility/appropriateness**

- Is the cost realistic?

- Is the equipment available?

- Is the methodology appropriate, and can data be obtained?

NB: A variable-indicator-methods matrix (VIM) should be elaborated to link up each variable to at least one indicator as well as the methods that will be used for data collection and analysis.

Example of a Variable-indicator-methods matrix (VIM)

Objectives	Variable	Measurement (indicator)	Method (data collection, analysis)	Sample size and type	Test statistics or other analysis	Reference literature if possible
Sub objective 1	Nutritional status	Body mass index	Anthropometric measurement	100	Z-score of weight/height index	Who does comments
		Body weight for age				
		Height for age				
	Mutual trust	openness	Interview, observation	50	Text accounting Life history quotations or experiences	Past events, historical recall, Kisoni, 2006
		Financial management	Interviews			
		honesty				
		Responsibility				
		Respectfulness				
		Transparency				

c. Research design

This relates to how the variables will be measured, how will the data be collected, the sampling design to be used and how the data will be analysed.

The chosen research design should be based on the nature and purpose/goal of the study.

Criteria for choosing a research design

- Determine the nature of the study:
    - purpose of the study : to establish correlation among variables or causation
    - correlation studies seek to understand, describe and predict occurrences or outcomes (desirable, undesirable)
        - exploratory (trying to understand certain relationships)
        - descriptive (trying to describe certain issues
        - analytical (focusing on testing hypotheses)
        - comparative
        - historical or narrative
        - etc.

- the study setting or environment: field (normal, natural occurrence of issue studied) or laboratory (artificial setting for occurrence)
- type of study: experimental (to establish causal connections) or correlational (to establish correlations).
    - an experimental design could be carried out either in the field or in the laboratory
    - Correlational studies are carried out in the natural environment – field.

- Degree of researcher's interference
    - Correlational studies have minimum researcher interference
    - Experimental design studies either have high researcher interference (in the case of laboratory experiment) or moderate interference (case of field experiments)

- Ability to manipulate variables (independent) and control other intervening factors that may affect the cause-effect relationship
- Time horizon:
    - Cross-sectional study: data collected only once during an investigation (one-shot)
    - Longitudinal study (collecting data more than once from the same system during the course of the study).

Experimental design mainly used:

Most research work is cross-sectional studies that are correlational, experimental or non-experimental, survey, exploratory, descriptive, analytical or historical.

Longitudinal studies need to be carried out repeatedly over a long period of time.

d. Sampling design

It refers to the process of selecting a smaller number of subjects from a larger population that the researcher is interested in studying or investigating.

Importance of sampling designed
- ✓ determines the type of generalisations that can be made from the findings of a research
- ✓ determines the usefulness and scientific nature of the research that has to be carried out

Three important elements in defining a sampling design
- ➤ sampling procedure
- ➤ Sampling criteria
- ➤ Sample size

i) Sampling procedure:

This refers to the method used in selecting the research sample or sample to be studied.

Two categories of sampling procedures: probability and nonprobability sampling.

Probability sampling:
- ensures that all the subjects required for the research have a probability (chance) of being selected
- Various types:
  - Simple random sampling (a known and equal chance); High level of generalizability
  - Systematic sampling (counting and choosing every subject that receives a certain number e.g. every 9th, 10th number or position)

  - Stratified random sampling (divide a study population into strata, then choose subjects from each stratum either using a simple random sampling or systematic sampling methods)

- Cluster sampling (a random selection of groups or clusters of subjects from the study population. Each cluster has an equal chance of being selected. All the subjects in each chosen cluster participate in the research or study. eg. Women, men, children farmers, handicaps, youths

- Area sampling: cluster sampling that is limited to a specific geographical area (country, city etc.)

Nonprobability sampling

Subjects of the research do not have a known probability or chance of being selected for the study.

It is used when the choice of subjects for the study involves only people who are in a position to give the required information.

e.g. sexual abuse, imprisonment, drug and alcohol addiction, widow and widowers, orphans etc.

Examples:

- Convenience sampling (collect data from whoever is available)
- Judgement sampling (select only subjects who are in the best position to provide the necessary data)
- Quota sampling (select people from different groups [underrepresented and highly represented] to make comparisons e.g. Cameroonian civil servants versus non-civil servants etc.

ii) Sampling criteria

It refers to stating the reasons for the choice of the research sample and/or sub samples.
It precises the relevance of the sample to the research

iii) Sample size

Too small or too large samples can distort the results of the research. A sample size depends on the population size and the issue at stake.

It is possible to choose sub samples from the main sample according to the type of information or data needed

e.   Research Methods

These refer to defining how the data will be collected and analysed.

In defining a research methodology, the following must be included:

+ A definition of the methods used ;

+ a step by step description of how the methods will be applied,;

+ the reason for the choice of each method used;

+ specify what each method is intended to measure; and

+ the limitations and strengths of each method to be used;

Criteria for selecting research methods:

➤ **Accuracy** (getting the correct answer). This includes:

- sensitivity;

- specificity

➤ **Precision (reliability, reproducibility, repeatability).**

➤ **Reliability:** ability of an instrument or method to accurately and stably measure a concept over time and across situations.

Data collection methods and their measurements

Some sources and methods for collecting data are:

i. Source: Secondary source; ii. Primary source

Secondary data:

Type of data collection: desktop study

- Method: Literature review

  + Gray literature (unpublished literature, reports etc.)

  + Publications, newspapers etc.

Primary data or empirical research:

Source: Subjects or people being researched

Methods:

+ Survey research

+ Observation

+ Interviews (structured, semi structured, unstructured)

+ Case study

+ Focus group and group interviews

+ Pairwise comparison

+ Pile sorting

+ Free listing

- Triad testing
- Census
- Data collection instruments:
- Questionnaires used for surveys and structured interviews
- Interview schedule used for unstructured and simple interviews, observations
- Checklist questions used for semi-structured interviews, observations
- Pictures
- Maps and mapping

Methods (ways) of administering research instruments:

- Face-to-face
- Self-administered
- Telephone interviews
- Internet based surveys and interviews
- Etc.

NB: Each method has its strengths and limitations; therefore a combination of methods is advisable.

Data analysis methods

- It concerns thinking over the type of analysis that will permit the obtaining of answers to the research questions raised. For each method specify:

  - What it is
  - Why choice of method and what results are you looking for
  - How to apply it

Specify:

  c) Statistical analysis (test-statistics) to be used and their measurements in case of quantitative data

  d) Other forms of qualitative analysis

Some methods of statistical data analysis include:

- Frequency counts⎤ for nominal (mutual exclusive groups)and ordinal scale (rank-order subjects)
- Chi-square (X^2) ⎦ data
- Mean
- Standard deviation
- Proportions
- Ratios
- Pearson correlation

- ➢ Spearman's correlation
- ➢ Regression and multiple regression analysis
- ➢ ANOVA

Some elements of qualitative data can be analysed using:

- ➢ Text analysis through process accounting
- ➢ Quotations
- ➢ Life histories
- ➢ Quantitative analysis through basic statistics (percentages, chi-square etc.)
- ➢ Graphs, picture presentations;
- ➢ Etc.

Interpretation and presentation of results

Results should be interpreted objectively to reduce any bias that will falsify the conclusions and generalisations made.

Interpretation should be based on the theoretical perspective (framework) and the topic of the research.

The explanations given should be valid.

The results could be presented in various forms:

e)	Graphics

f)	Text

g)	Tables

h)	etc.

Expected Results

It refers to translating the objectives into output or what we want to obtain (desired situation). This section is optional.

Chronogram

It is an indication of the length of time that each stage of the research will take.

It highlights the proposed tasks and stages and times for their completion.

It may be presented in form of:

- ➤ A timeline
- ➤ A chart
- ➤ A flowchart
- ➤ Etc.

NB: Elaborating a time line and charting helps in identifying which activities can be carried out at the same time.

Example of a chronogram in chart form:

ACTIVITY	February 2017	March 2017	May 2017	June 2017	July 2017	August 2017	September2017	March 2015	April 2014	May 2014	June 2014	July 2014	Aug. 2014
Elaborating research topic	▰												
Literature review	▰▰▰▰▰▰												
Elaborating research proposal	▰▰												

Research Budget

Bibliography or References

Every source of grey and published literature used must be included in the reference list at the end of the document.

The **Harvard referencing style** is accepted by (the University).

- ➤ It involves in-text citations using parentheses. e.g. Author's surname, year of publication. Page numbers included if citation is taken from a small section of the document.
- ➤ Enter or use the author's last name (Surname, Family name) in the reference list and abbreviate the other names i.e. first and/or middle name(s).
- ➤ Entries in the reference list should follow an alphabetical order

- ➤ The reference layout, capitalisation and punctuation used must be consistent.
- ➤ The format used in the reference list varies according to the type of literature source referred to.
  - Books
  - Book chapters
  - Journal Articles
  - Patent
  - Article from a database
  - Website articles
  - Etc.

➤ **Books:** Surname, Initial(s). Date. *Title*. Edition. Place of Publication: Publisher. (Series.)

Example 1: Book with a single author:

➤ Philip, A. 1995. *It is too late*. 2nd Edition. Seattle: Miche bozley.

Example 2: Book with 2 to 6 authors:

➤ Giggs, J. S., Poneman, D. B. & Gallucci, R. L. 2004. *Going critical : the first North Korean nuclear crisis*. Washington, D.C.: Brookings Institution Press

Example 3: Book with more than 6 authors:

➤ Rogder, K., Rodeshell, J., Fulton, L., Lochhead, M., Craig, K., Peterson, R., et.al. 1967. *Brain cells and insect behavior*. Cambridge, MA: Harvard University Press.

➤ **Book Chapters:** Surname, Initial(s). Date. Chapter title, in *Book Title,* edited by Editor first name. Editor Surname. Place of Publication: Publisher: Pages in book.

Example:

➤ Faxter, M. 1976. Social class and health inequalities, in *Equalities and inequalities in health,* edited by Carl J. Carter. London: Academic Press: 120-135.

➤ **Journal Articles:** Surname, Initial(s). Date. Title of article. *Title of Periodical*, volume (issue number): page numbers.

Example:

➤ Norton, N. 1996. Health and safety in outdoor activity centres. *Journal of Adventure Education and Outdoor Leadership*, 12(4): 8-9.

➤ **Patent:** Name(s) of inventor(s). Date of issue. *Title of Patent*, Number of Patent including country of issue.

Example:

➢ Smith, P. L. 2002. *Particle trap for compressed gas insulated transmission systems*, US Patent 4554399.

➢ **Article from a Database:** Surname, Initials. Date. Article Title. *Journal Title*, volume (issue number): page numbers. (Date accessed, from Database).

➢ *Example:*

➢ Sopensky, E. 2002. Chocolate makes money, *Business Journal*. 3(1): 20-24. (accessed April 14, 2004, from ProQuest database).

Website: Bibliographic details are arranged in the sequence:

➢ Surname, initial(s). Date (last updated). *Title and Website*. [Online]. Publisher. Available: URL. [Date you accessed the site].

➢ *Example:*
➢ Dawson, J., Deubert, K., Grey-Smith, S. & Smith, L. 2002. *'S' Trek 6: Referencing, not plagiarism*. [Online]. Available: http://lisweb.curtin.edu.au/guides/studytrekk/strek6.html. [4 September 2004] .